INCREDIBLY

By
Nina Canault

Series director :
François Cherrier

SMALL

New
Discovery
BOOKS
New York

Change scale to see the infinitely tiny.

If we limited ourselves to just what our eyes can see, we would miss many marvelous things, for in fact the world of the visible is only a minuscule part of what exists! Our imaginations, rich as they are, can never equal the wonders of reality: The microscopic world, highly organized, conceals easily as much beauty as exists in our world. To see the incredibly tiny is to change scale and enter a new dimension where the existence of many beings challenges our concept of reality and our common sense. For example, how could we ever imagine that the fossilized skeletons of microscopic animals dissolved by the sea could reform and reappear 150 million years later? Or that the antennas of most ordinary insects are covered with feathers . . . or that our hair is covered with scales?

These test tubes contain human blood, and the scanning electronic microscope (SEM) has isolated a red corpuscle from it. Each corpuscle measures about 7.5 microns in diameter (one micron equals 4/100,000 of an inch). The images obtained by using the SEM are always in black and white. Afterward these microscopic images are tinted (as here in red) in order to give the object being studied its original color.

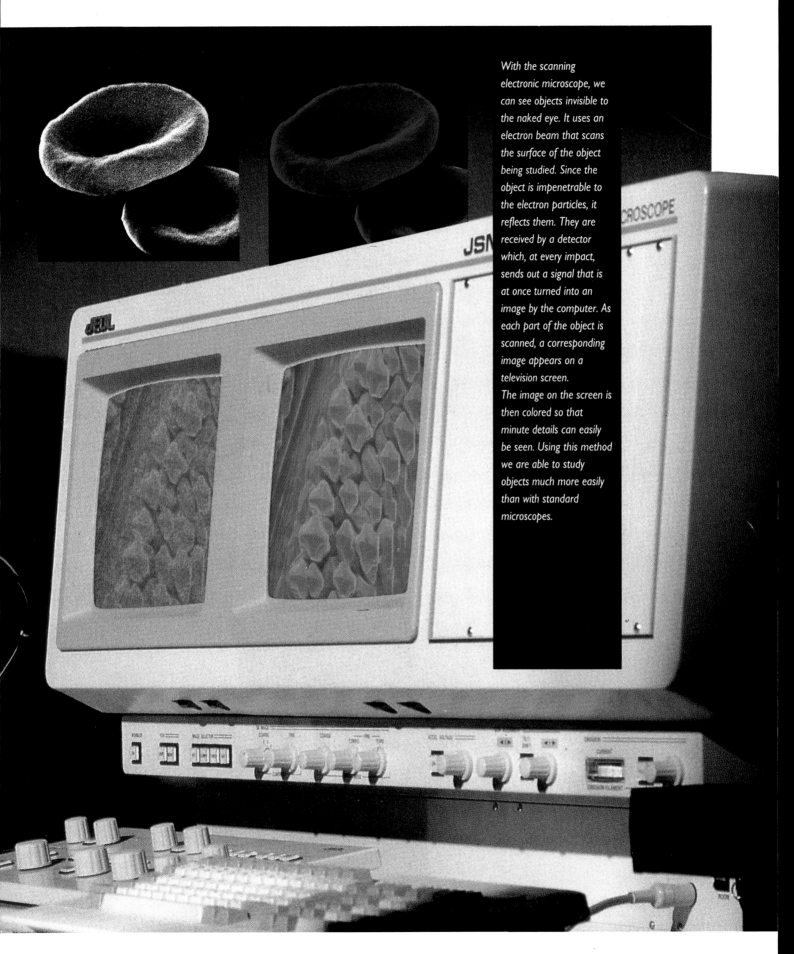

With the scanning electronic microscope, we can see objects invisible to the naked eye. It uses an electron beam that scans the surface of the object being studied. Since the object is impenetrable to the electron particles, it reflects them. They are received by a detector which, at every impact, sends out a signal that is at once turned into an image by the computer. As each part of the object is scanned, a corresponding image appears on a television screen. The image on the screen is then colored so that minute details can easily be seen. Using this method we are able to study objects much more easily than with standard microscopes.

A fresh eye on our everyday existence

The everyday existence that we think we know so well has many surprises in store for us . . . salt and sugar grains that we think are round become cubical or rectangular; calcium salt, that unpleasant white crust that forms on dishes, is transformed into an elegantly flowered oriental rug; the metal that we thought was smooth and solid is in fact a composition of imperfect crystals. As for the dust in our houses and the fur of our dogs, they metamorphose into thick, impenetrable forests!

What can this group of cubes be? A model of a scene from a movie featuring a new type of spaceship? No, simply sea salt cultivated in a laboratory, magnified 341 times.

WHEN A ROUND GRAIN HIDES CRYSTAL CUBES

Salt and sugar . . . they are part of our daily lives, and yet we scarcely see them. What do you think about when you are putting salt on your egg or sugar in your tea? No doubt lots of things—but you're probably not thinking about the real shape of those grains you're so busy sprinkling on your food or about their unusual history!

These are not roughly hewn stones . . .

these are table salt crystals!

Common salt has been used by man for his food needs since our earliest times. Seawater contains an average of 4.2 ounces per gallon. Enlarged 100 times, these grains of salt take on the form of cubes. Their edges have probably been rounded during manufacturing in order to prevent them from sticking to one another. Our table salt contains 99% sodium chloride. The 1% that remains is composed of sodium sulfate and magnesium chloride, two elements that extract moisture and thereby allow salt to flow freely. In certain civilizations, organisms that need salt every day to compensate for water loss consume much more than those in others: the Japanese use 1 to 1.5 ounces of salt a day, while we only use about .35 ounce on the average! Salt is necessary for us, but we shouldn't overindulge because too much salt can be one of the causes of arterial hypertension.

WHEN A ROUND GRAIN HIDES RECTANGULAR CRYSTALS

Sugar is a liquid substance extracted from two main vegetables: beets and sugarcane. During the refining process, this substance, having been purified and bleached, crystallizes and solidifies. Sugar is a member of the glycoside family. Its chemical name is sucrose. Beet sugar is white; cane sugar is more or less brown depending on how much it has been refined. The crystals can be small or large and can be made into cubes, grains, or powder. There is also corn syrup, used to make cakes and drinks. The sugar called rock candy is obtained by slow evaporation and resembles small yellowish transparent "rocks."

Sugarcane crystals, taken from a package of grain sugar, enlarged 48 times. Cane sugar is brown because it hasn't been refined as much as beet sugar and so still contains some impurities. It tastes quite different.

Sucrose and glucose, found in candies, pastries, and soft drinks, are those rapidly digested glycosides that dieticians hate. However, they play an important role when the body needs to make a special effort in a short period of time because they release energy that can be used immediately.

7

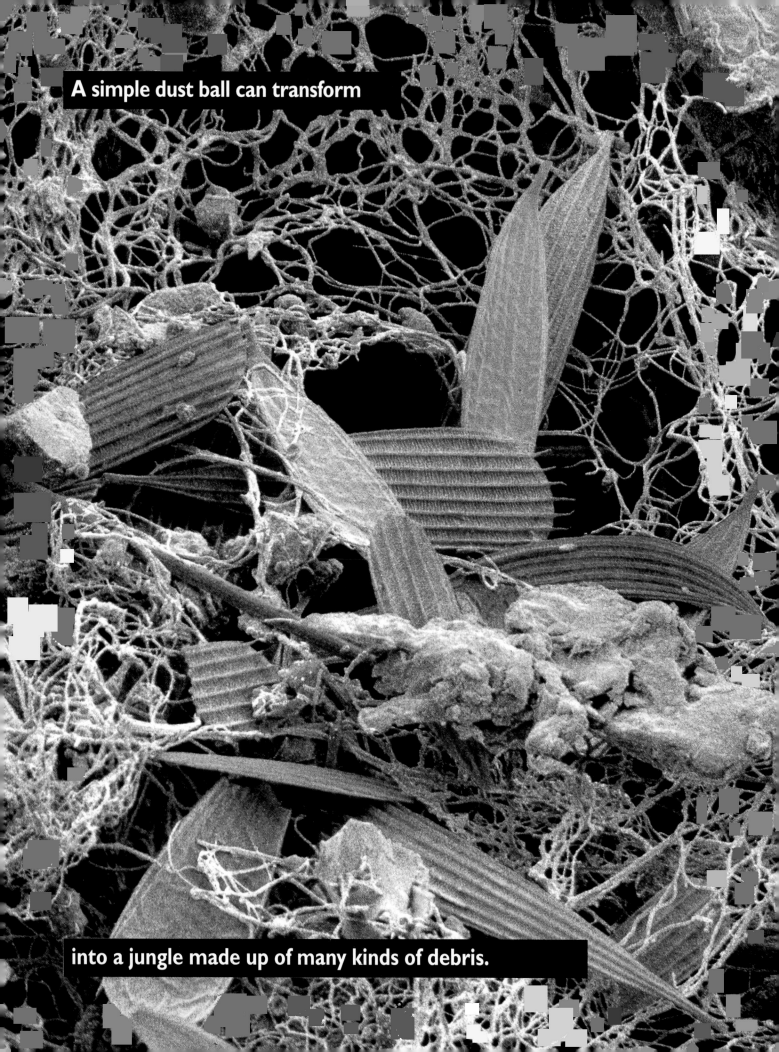

A simple dust ball can transform

into a jungle made up of many kinds of debris.

DUST, CEMETERY, OR ATTIC?

Here's a view of part of a blanket enlarged 5,000 times. Dust is mixed with wool fibers and shreds of spiderwebs (the white tangled filaments), remains of vegetables (the green), and insect debris (the orange and yellow). Below right, isolated debris of insect shells.

This tiny crab louse is busily digging through a forest of household debris. He is trying to get as much done as he can before being sucked up by a vacuum cleaner! An unwanted houseguest, he makes his home in the dust on the floors.

The house is an ecosystem containing people, their pets, and their plants, as well as small insects, microscopic algae, and mold. But the dust of a house is also an ecosystem—this one microscopic. It's a whole environment made up of the residue of its different "populations," whether mineral, vegetable, or animal. House dust contains within it a mosaic of living creatures, many dependent on others (such as molds or bacteria). It also contains right in our own houses remains of this multiplicity of life—often secret—which moves and swarms all the time just under our feet: vegetable remains, minuscule pieces of glass, hair, and scales. Those dust balls that our vacuum cleaners go after without mercy are perhaps the debris of monstrous fights between microscopic animals, ticks against moths for example! At the very least, some of these creatures must certainly have made a tasty meal for some wandering spider! The dust of a house doesn't have the same inhabitants and elements in it year-round. It, too, like the beings and things that compose it, changes according to the season. Changes in the temperature outside or in the humidity changes the beings and things that grow and live in the dust balls. But no matter what the season, there is always a mixture of vegetable, mineral, and animal debris in our dust!

The dust ball is a grayish cottony accumulation that can be found in all the small hidden corners of our houses. But this ordinary dust ball—isn't it also a vestige of the past? An attic, a gallery of portraits of innumerable beings that we pass by all the time without seeing? It might make those who love to clean house pause a moment in their scrubbing and dusting!

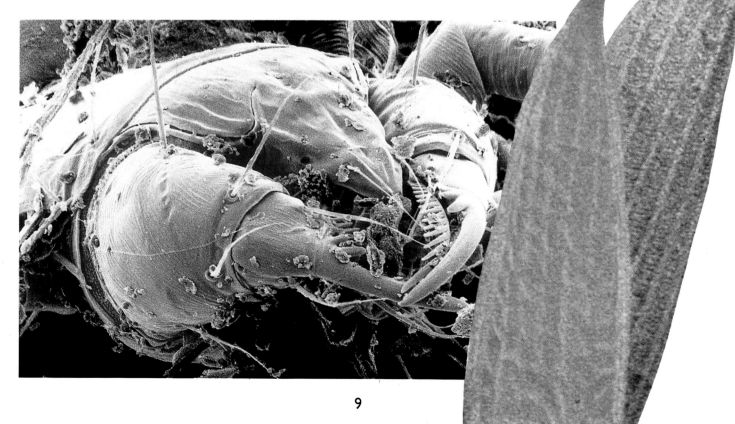

THE SCALES THAT COVER HAIR AND FUR . . .

Some things that don't really move, that remain inert, still seem to be living things. This is the case with fingernails, the outer layer of skin, and hairs. However, these specialized tissues are very strange cases—they are both living *and* dead! Hair, for example, with its smooth brilliant appearance, its thickness, and its vibrant movement would seem to tell us it is living. But the part of the hair we actually see is dead. It is a hollow sort of stem bristling with minuscule scales that cover it entirely. Only the root is living.

Just as we lose hair every day, we also lose skin. Our bodies get rid of about .1 ounce of skin daily. And the whole skin is entirely renewed every three weeks! On an average, the human body loses a total of 40 to 48 pounds of dead cells during a lifetime.

Skin hairs, like the hairs on our head, also have cells that multiply. As these cells move up toward the surface of the skin, they synthesize keratin, the tough fibrous protein forming the impermeable outer layer of skin. Each hair has a microscopic muscle so it can stand up, with or without the others! It's this tiny muscle that is working when we get goose bumps!

How long does hair live? Each strand of hair has a period of growth that lasts from 3 to 7 years. During this time the hair grows regularly at about .014 inch a day (with an average diameter of .003 inch). There is a sudden halt in growth. This dormant period lasts several weeks, and finally the strand of hair falls out. Immediately a new hair begins to grow. A normal head of hair consists of 100,000 to 250,000 strands. We lose hair all year, about a hundred strands a day on the average. This is perfectly natural and doesn't hurt the hair at all. The growth cycle of the scalp is not related to the seasons, unlike the molting or shedding of animal fur.

This collie is like all long-haired dogs in that it has two molting periods a year: its fur gets more resilient and thicker at the onset of cold weather, but with the coming of warmer weather, it begins to lose some of its thickness. However, the physiology of domestic animals is modified by their contact with humans. Those dogs who live in warm houses or apartments and are not therefore subject to extreme temperature changes tend to lose their hair just as we do—a little every day!

This is not a tropical forest at sunset,

This is a microscopic photo of a dog's skin and hair follicles, enlarged 855 times. Long-haired dogs, as we can see here, have an undergrowth of fur: a kind of downy hair. This down forms with the coming of winter and falls out in the spring as soon as it warms up outside.

it's the fur of a very well-groomed dog!

THE INFINITELY TINY . . . TECHNOLOGICALLY

When technology talks about chips, it's not a reference to potato chips but to the most up-to-date scientific discovery of today: the microchip or microelectronic. Whether hidden in a car, a washing machine, an automatic teller machine, a home computer, a pocket calculator, a magnetic card, or a watch, the micro-chip transmits all one's orders. It proves the old saying about great things often coming from small packages.

The chip or microprocessor is the organ of command. It commands a machine tool, a CD Player, a calculator. Specifically, it's a microscopic bit of silicon crystal onto which many electronic components—called transistors—have been mounted in order to create what are called integrated circuits. The chip is the basic component of the computer. Although the human neuron stays the same size from generation to generation, the same is not true of electronic material, which, because of technological advances, races toward greater and greater miniaturization. Thanks to the micro-chip, the simplest pocket calculator of today is more powerful than those enormous calculators (covering an area of 1,615 square feet) that were first used in the United States in 1945. Miniaturization today is synonymous with progress, and modern technology has not yet revealed all its secrets. . . .

Several dozen years ago the first microchip measured .28 inch across and integrated 2,300 transistors. Today, a telephone card (or credit card) with a chip of .12 inch holds 72,000 transistors! A quartz watch contains 5,000 chips, a pocket calculator 20,000, and the simple disk drive of a computer, 100,000!

In the photo opposite, we can compare two organs in command of a function (enlarged 687 times). The first is organic; the second is not. One is a human neuron (in yellow); the other is an electronic chip (in mauve). The extensions of the cerebral cell, the axons, are, on the average, the size of several dozen microns. The neuron has been placed on a chip that is only a small fraction of an inch in size.

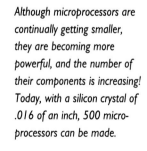

Although microprocessors are continually getting smaller, they are becoming more powerful, and the number of their components is increasing! Today, with a silicon crystal of .016 of an inch, 500 micro-processors can be made.

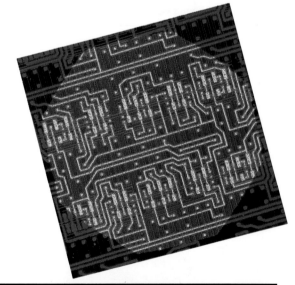

An incredibly tiny thing, but incredibly efficient.

EMPTY OR FULL?

Polystyrene is a plastic insulator, obtained by a chemical process called polymerization using styrene, a product that comes from oil. Polystyrene was invented in 1843 and today is omnipresent in our environment, especially these days when energy conservation is considered of prime importance.

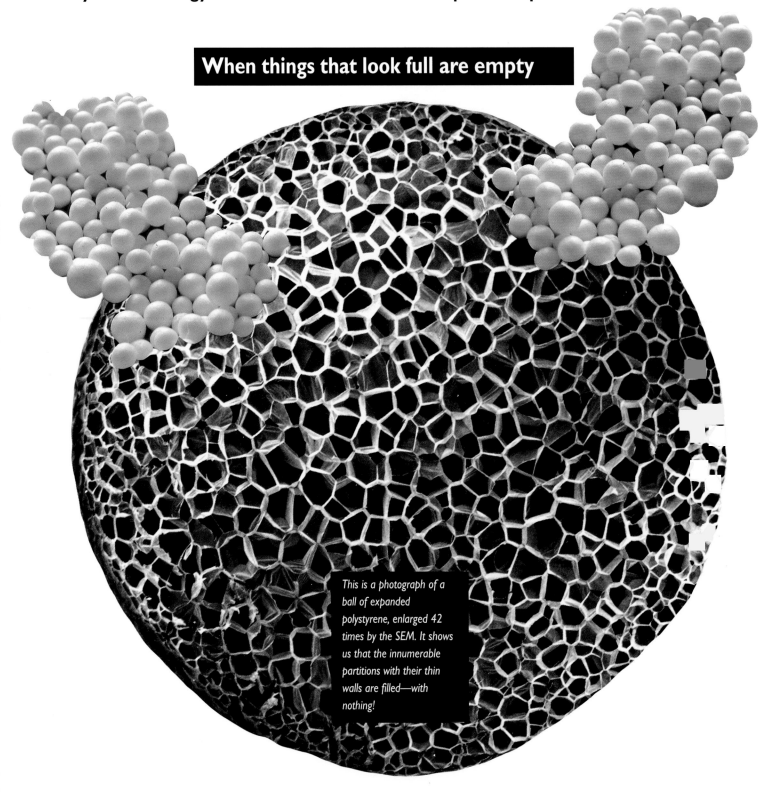

When things that look full are empty

This is a photograph of a ball of expanded polystyrene, enlarged 42 times by the SEM. It shows us that the innumerable partitions with their thin walls are filled—with nothing!

SMOOTH OR LINED?

Just like animals and vegetables, metals are born and grow! It is possible to watch this growth thanks to the SEM by analyzing some metal samples, all made of crystals, while they are solidifying. You can then see them forming and coming together. The aluminum ingot below is traced with easily seen, those that make up metals are microscopic. In a single cubic inch there are about 16.4 million, with differing geometric configurations. Aluminum, which is a very light metal, is often mixed with magnesium, copper, zinc, and silicon to improve its physical properties, especially its resistance to bending.

When things that look smooth are rough

designs and relief that reflects the crystalline nature of combined metals. These irregularities also come about from the difficult processes of melting the metal in the casting mold and then cooling it. The metal's texture will differ according to how little or long it is left to solidify.

Unlike natural rock crystals such as quartz where the crystals are large and

The surface of an aluminum ingot enlarged 300 times. Metals—and aluminum in particular—always seem to be very smooth, so we should expect to see a totally flat surface. But all those marks deeply ingrained in the metal remind us of its crystalline composition!

The tiny world of plants

How do you recognize a vegetable? At first thought, the answer seems simple: Vegetables are usually green. But if we look closer—through a microscope—we can discover the secrets of a plant's beginnings, its biological structure, its architecture, or its organs—all things we cannot see with the naked eye and that we miss otherwise. A close look at the vegetable world reveals the extraordinary spectacle of its limitless adaptation to the environment.

This rug decorated with tiny shields is actually the reverse side of a leaf from an ornamental Japanese shrub: eleagans pungens maculata, enlarged 90 times (above). The down that covers these leaves protects the pores, or stomata, of the plant, through which the essential gases and water vapors pass. These tiny shields catch and hold the air along the surface of the leaf, thus creating a microclimate. The process is much like the loss of water through transpiration.

MILLIONS OF TINY MOUTHS!

The mouths of our skin! This is a photo of the palm of a hand, enlarged 612 times. The small crater is an excessive swelling of the pore due to a blister. Pores are minuscule openings on the skin that release, among other things, secretions of the sudoriferous glands, better known as sweat. If the outside temperature rises, our bodies secrete a lot of sweat, which reduces body heat and gives moisture back to the dry skin.

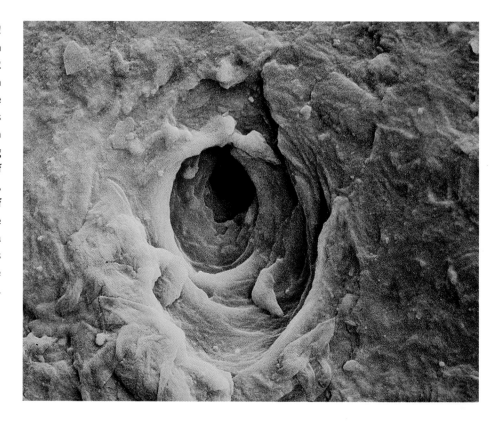

Bottom left: The leaf of a rose bush, enlarged about 500 times, with open stomates. Their action is controlled by two "watch cells" on either side. When the cells fill with water, the stomates open to release excess moisture.

Right: Closed stomates on an elder leaf, enlarged about 500 times.

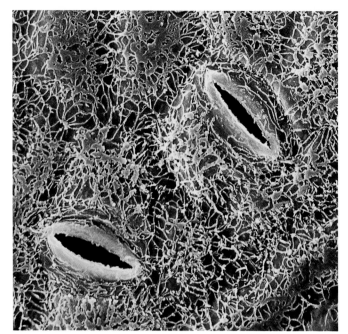

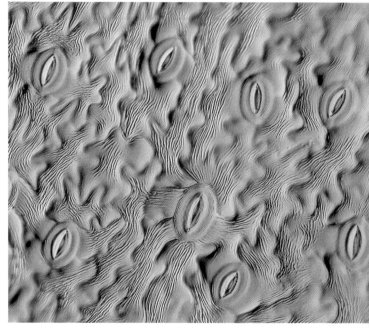

When the mouths open . . .

A close-up of the surface of a tobacco leaf, enlarged 985 times. The plant breathes through its pores, the stomata, which is its way of gathering the organic material for its nourishment. When the pores close, it's a natural phenomenon due to darkness or to dryness. Two pilot cells situated on either side of the pore opening control the dilation: when they are swollen with water, the pore opens; when they dry up, the pore closes.

At night, plants breathe as we do, inhaling oxygen from the air and exhaling carbon dioxide. But during the day the exchange of gases produces the opposite effect. The chlorophyll present in plant leaves acts as a solar battery—it captures light energy, which allows it to absorb the carbon dioxide from the air. The gas is then broken down into carbon, which it retains, and oxygen, which it rejects. This process is called photosynthesis. It only happens during the day. At night, there is only respiration.

Mouths for volcanoes! Often dangerous or even deadly for humans and at the same time fascinating when they spit out their lava, these volcano craters might be termed the mouths of our planet!

Breathing is possible only for advanced organisms such as humans, animals, and plants. The science of evolution, phylogeny, which tries to establish a genealogical tree of the species, gives a major place to plants. Plants are the original producers of living material, the sources of life in our world. For example, forests alone each year produce about 60 billion of the 180 billion tons of organic material produced on the planet, or 11.6 tons per acre per year. This is why it is so vitally important to protect our environment and especially our forests.

DIVING INTO THE HEART OF WOOD

There is the tree and there is wood. And make no mistake about it—both are living: life pulsates in leaves, flowers, and fruits, of course, but also in wood. Wood has always been a valuable material. And because it is living material and not dead, it varies considerably, both in substance and in appearance. Sometimes variations take place even in the same piece of wood. Wood is also unstable—it changes according to humidity or dryness. Used in its original solid state, it deteriorates, buckles, warps, and never stops being under stress. In the past it was used to build houses and the frameworks of important buildings. Wood is still very much used—we can hardly do without it— but it has changed! Once, solid rustic wood, full of knotholes and fissures, with strength only perpendicular to its grain, was most common, but now it is the reconstituted woods that are most used, being better suited to today's needs. Furniture catalogs advertise primarily these new woods: plywood, veneer, pressboard, particle board. The principle is simple: The wood is cut in small pieces that are assembled by orienting the wood fibers perpendicularly or randomly to one another. This process makes wood more resistant to pressure or stress.

The photograph opposite shows a horizontal cross-section of a tree trunk. A tree's age can easily be calculated by counting the different circular rings that begin at the heart and continue to the edge. Each ring is the result of a new bark—a sort of molting—and represents 10 years.

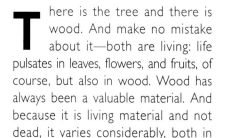

A piece of birch plywood in cross section and enlarged 165 times. This wood has been attacked by a microscopic mushroom, the Serpula lachrymans. The cylindrical cells that we see in the image are the "veins," which carry the sap throughout the trunk and connect the different parts of the tree.

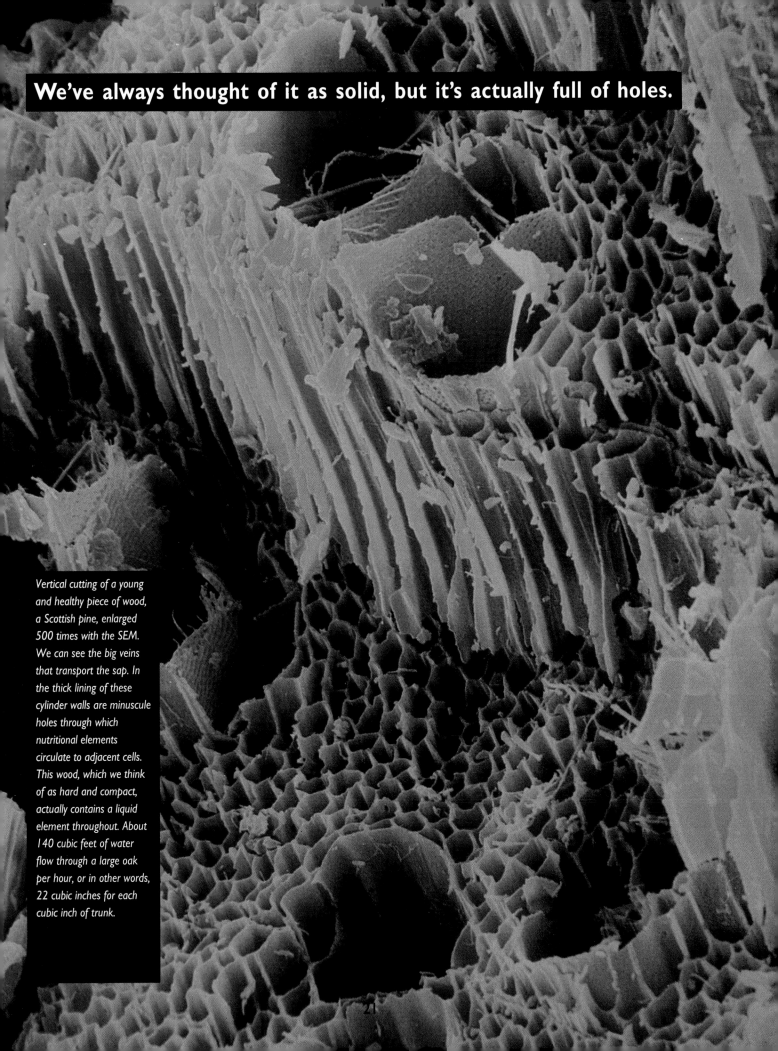

We've always thought of it as solid, but it's actually full of holes.

Vertical cutting of a young and healthy piece of wood, a Scottish pine, enlarged 500 times with the SEM. We can see the big veins that transport the sap. In the thick lining of these cylinder walls are minuscule holes through which nutritional elements circulate to adjacent cells. This wood, which we think of as hard and compact, actually contains a liquid element throughout. About 140 cubic feet of water flow through a large oak per hour, or in other words, 22 cubic inches for each cubic inch of trunk.

THESE MUSHROOMS WE LOVE SO MUCH!

Although fleas, moths, and other such "friendly" insects are as familiar guests to us as cats and dogs, they are definitely unwanted ones! However, it's even harder to imagine that we can be the prey of plants!

A togetherness more or less equal

There are many things that we don't know about the wide variety of plants known under the common name of "mushrooms." The reason is that most of the 150,000 known species are microscopic, living in the soil and in the water. The best known mushrooms, the ones we see growing in forests for example, represent only a few hundred of the species. However, whether macroscopic or microscopic, these plants, unlike others, cannot use energy from the sun to produce the material necessary for their life: they do not carry out the process of photosynthesis. Even though they are often grouped with algae, their behavior, reproduction, and method of nourishment defy scholarly classifications: the characteristics of these species fall somewhere between those of the animal kingdom and of the plant kingdom! Incapable of existing through the process of photosynthesis, mushrooms have had to develop other ways to survive. Some have chosen the road of "enlightened parasitism," living off a host while treating it with great care as one would treat a chicken laying golden eggs. An example is that of the mummy of Ramses II (1300–234 B.C.). Scientists, by means of sophisticated chemical and physical analyses, discovered that no fewer than 96 species of microscopic fungi had infested the mummy of the Pharaoh. Other mushrooms feed by

decomposing dead plant material—or animal material! In 1929 the Englishman Alexander Fleming discovered penicillin, used in the treatment of many infections, by observing preparations contaminated by mold and isolating from them a fungus, the *Penicillium notatum,* which secretes an antimicrobial substance.

Opposite: a microscopic fungus enlarged 1,026 times, the Aspergillus niger, commonly present in our environment, especially in dust, earth, and plant material. The blue filaments are hyphae (to the naked eye they often look like mold), which hold the spores—here shown as brown balls—that allow the fungus to reproduce. The Aspergillus niger sometimes lives off man as a parasite. It can infest the inner ear, provoking mycosis with inflammation of the canal leading to the eardrum. Above, in insertion: a colony of yeast enlarged 925 times. Yeast is composed of single-celled fungi that reproduce by budding. They are found in our digestive tube but fortunately are useful and beneficial.

MARVELOUS POLLEN!

When the season for flowers comes, the wind and the insects have the job of transporting pollen, minuscule fertile grains, from the stamen, or male organs, to the pistil, or female organs. The atmosphere is therefore periodically—and especially in the spring—full of these microscopic particles responsible for allergies in one out of every ten people!

The openings we see here are the pores and very sculpted ridges of the germinal furrows. The external wall of a grain of pollen, the exine, is composed of a material that is thought to be the most resistant of any living material. A single plant is able to produce billions of grains of pollen.

Thanks to these different photos of pollen, we can see the great diversity of forms of these tiny balls of dust, which vary in size from 2.5 to 200 microns.

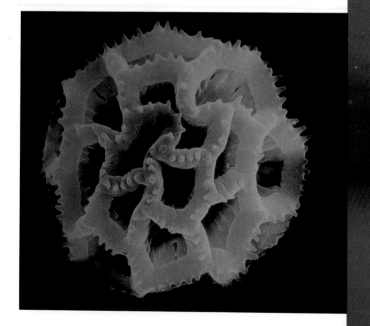

The smallest grains in the world

The grain of pollen contains the male seed of the flower. Carried by the wind or by an insect, it lands on the upper part of the pistil or stigma, where it germinates. Then a small tube grows out of the germ or from a pore of the grain of pollen and penetrates the stigma to reach the ovule. After that, the male nucleus travels through the tube to fertilize the ovule, where the seed is then formed. The bee below has just gathered the nectar of the flower. The bee is thus participating in pollination.

We vaguely imagine pollen as a multitude of small round grains. In reality, there is an immense variety of form among pollens, and this has enabled scientists to classify plants, each pollen being a sort of signature of a group of plants. Scientists have recorded 24 types of pollen made up of extremely robust grains that have the curious characteristic of being able to encrust themselves in large quantities into rock. Sediments, peat, clay, limestone, coal, and fine sand have held them prisoner for centuries. This exceptional resistance to the vagaries of time has allowed researchers from the French National Center of Scientific Research to ascertain that forests of oak and white heath were already plentiful on the Languedoc coast 6,000 years before our era! The study of pollen, palynology, has enabled us to reconstruct the climatic and ecological conditions associated with the evolution of life on earth. It can go back as far as 465,000 years.

The sea, cradle of the incredibly small

The seas and oceans contain great numbers of plankton floating on the surface of the water. Scientists think that certain planktonic beings have a biological makeup that would place them in the animal kingdom and that others, to the contrary, seem to be closer to the plant kingdom. This is the distinction between zooplankton and phytoplankton. The diatoms, tiny single-celled algae, are the most important of the phytoplankton.

Samples of zooplankton and phytoplankton, enlarged 6 times. Many marine animals feed on plankton: sardines, anchovies, sprats and mackerels, herrings and whales, all of which filter the water using the spiny extensions of their branchiae or their plates of baleen.

THE SECRETS OF ZOOPLANKTON

Because the word *plankton* comes from the ancient Greek *planktos*, which means wandering, it is generally thought that planktonic animals drift with the current and do not govern their own movements. But are they really adrift?

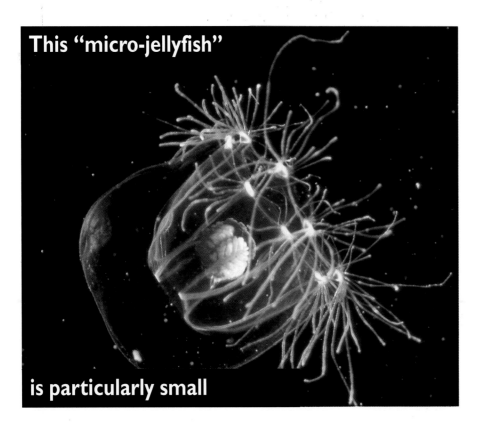

This "micro-jellyfish" is particularly small

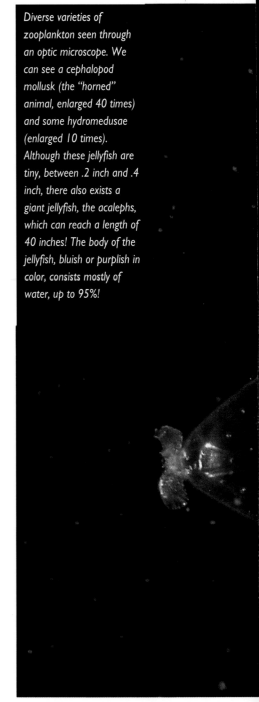

Diverse varieties of zooplankton seen through an optic microscope. We can see a cephalopod mollusk (the "horned" animal, enlarged 40 times) and some hydromedusae (enlarged 10 times). Although these jellyfish are tiny, between .2 inch and .4 inch, there also exists a giant jellyfish, the acalephs, which can reach a length of 40 inches! The body of the jellyfish, bluish or purplish in color, consists mostly of water, up to 95%!

A zooplankton is able to travel vertically. It feeds from phytoplankton—the plant plankton—which is present above it in the upper strata of the ocean exposed to light. Therefore, the zooplankton climbs toward the surface during the night and goes back down during the day. Once on the surface, these vertical migrations also enable it to move horizontally over great distances, carried by the currents, which are more rapid than in the ocean depths. It's thought that these tiny animals can change their habitat because after having been carried a certain distance by the current, they descend into a different environment.

This movement would tend to support the theory that the zooplankton's floating is not in fact random but deliberate.

The phytoplankton is the first link of the food chain that governs the seas, and the zooplankton the second. A ton of phytoplankton is necessary to feed only 220 pounds of copepods (zooplankton). These 220 pounds of copepods feed in their turn 22 pounds of herring, which, eaten by a tuna, enable it to gain 2.2 pounds. As for man, he only gains 3.5 ounces by eating 2.2 pounds of tuna!

Hydromedusae have cells containing stinging poison, the cnidoblastes. With their long tentacles filled with this poison, they paralyze their victims. These tiny transparent animals are in fact insatiable carnivores!

The large zooplankton family also includes a variety of small shrimp called krill. Krill measure .2 inch to 2 inches and feed upon diatoms, minuscule algae. Whales are particularly fond of these shrimp and eat an enormous amount of them.

WHEN THE PLANKTON DRESSES UP . . .

The Radiolaria in the photograph on the left (enlarged 6,750 times) is of the species Haliomma, and the one in the photograph on the right (enlarged 1,750 times) belongs to the Rhizophaera family. They both belong to the order of Spumellaires (from "spume," which means "frothy"). We see here only the siliceous skeletons of the two animals. Their mineral skeletal structure is isolated from the marine environment by a cellular membrane that extends into the tentacles. The spines that we see here could be considered the "bones" of the tentacles.

The beautiful geodesic dome in the Villette Park in Paris, whose structure was made by assembling many triangular aluminum plates on a metallic framework. Inside is a movie theater that shows images projected on a semispherical screen 10,764 square feet in size, the largest in the world!

Thanks to these fascinating photographs, we are able to see that the forms existing in nature are in no way inferior to those created in our modern world and can be a source of inspiration to our architects.

The Radiolaria are part of the large zooplankton family but are different from the creatures on the two preceding pages because of their exterior "skeleton" that protects their body. Although they aren't plants, they nevertheless need light to live, and benefit from the photosynthesis that takes place in the zooanthelles, single-celled algae even smaller then the creatures who live off them. These algae provide their hosts with easy food in exchange for a certain protection. The radiolarian has more of an animal nature but is not a hunter. It simply floats, and when a small prey comes within its reach, seizes it using one of its many tentacles (called pseudopods). Passively buffeted about in a horizontal direction by the sea currents, the radiolarian's only active way of moving is vertically, using its central capsule containing vesicles filled with a sort of oil. Lighter than water, this oil enables it to move up easily to the surface. To go back down, it expels the oil. Radiolaria often live in colonies held together by gelatin. These colonies, spherical or filamentous, can reach a length of 16 feet. They are extremely voracious: They've been known to eat shellfish larva, and even big jellyfish!

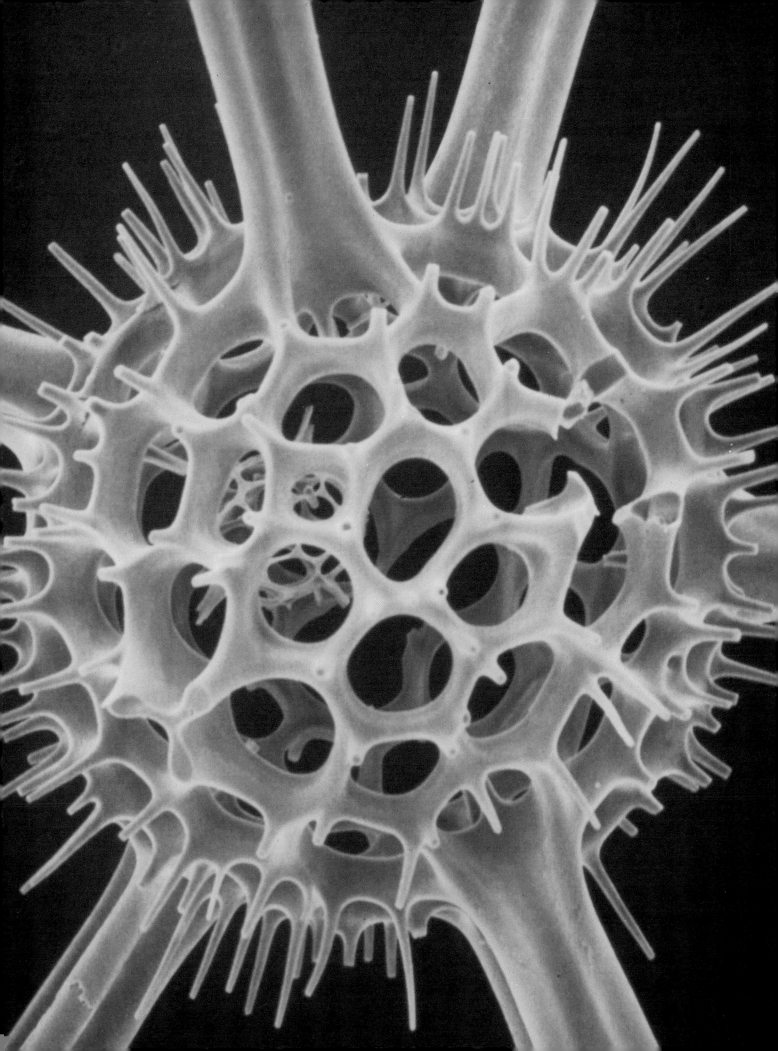

WHEN THE PLANKTON DIES . . .

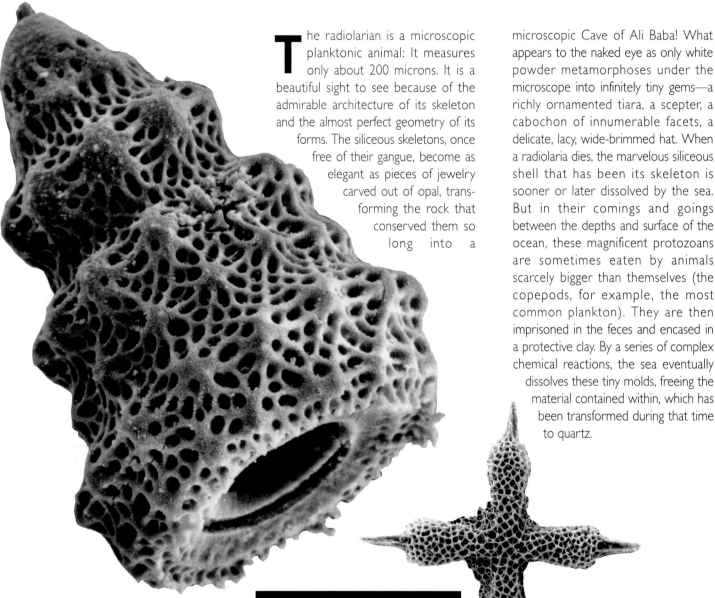

The radiolarian is a microscopic planktonic animal: It measures only about 200 microns. It is a beautiful sight to see because of the admirable architecture of its skeleton and the almost perfect geometry of its forms. The siliceous skeletons, once free of their gangue, become as elegant as pieces of jewelry carved out of opal, transforming the rock that conserved them so long into a microscopic Cave of Ali Baba! What appears to the naked eye as only white powder metamorphoses under the microscope into infinitely tiny gems—a richly ornamented tiara, a scepter, a cabochon of innumerable facets, a delicate, lacy, wide-brimmed hat. When a radiolaria dies, the marvelous siliceous shell that has been its skeleton is sooner or later dissolved by the sea. But in their comings and goings between the depths and surface of the ocean, these magnificent protozoans are sometimes eaten by animals scarcely bigger than themselves (the copepods, for example, the most common plankton). They are then imprisoned in the feces and encased in a protective clay. By a series of complex chemical reactions, the sea eventually dissolves these tiny molds, freeing the material contained within, which has been transformed during that time to quartz.

This radiolarian fossil, named Novixitus, is one of the order of Nacellaires (in the form of a hoop net). It is 90 million years old and was discovered in Rumania by the geologist Paulian Dumitrica.

The oldest known radiolarian fossil carries its 500 million years well! Geologists are always looking for such fossils in order to date the great evolutionary periods of our planet. In these 500 million years, innumerable species have developed and then disappeared. Miraculously, some of them have left their skeletons behind them, encrusted in the rocky sediments. Radiolaria fossils have even been found in the Alps, where some 150 million years ago there was a sea!

This superbly latticed cross measures about 500 microns. It's been enlarged 790 times. It's not the royal locket of some tiny queen but the skeleton of a 190-million-year-old radiolarian fossil! It is called Crucella mijo De Vewer, named for the French researcher who discovered and isolated it in 1981. It was found in a big limestone formation in a mountain in Turkey and belongs to the order of the Spumellaires.

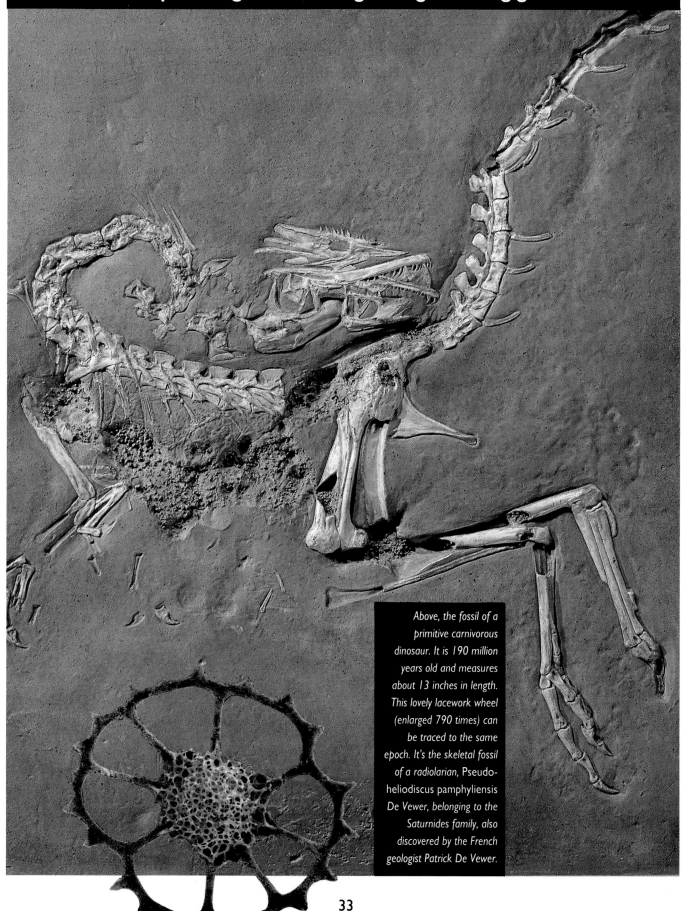

Above, the fossil of a primitive carnivorous dinosaur. It is 190 million years old and measures about 13 inches in length. This lovely lacework wheel (enlarged 790 times) can be traced to the same epoch. It's the skeletal fossil of a radiolarian, Pseudo-heliodiscus pamphyliensis De Vewer, belonging to the Saturnides family, also discovered by the French geologist Patrick De Vewer.

THE SECRETS OF PHYTOPLANKTON

Life on earth is only possible because there exists, among other things, a succession of food chains. In the seas and oceans many of these food chains begin with phytoplankton, which convert solar energy into living matter. These same microscopic plants produce two thirds of the world's oxygen and participate, following the example of bacteria, in the purification of water. The sea is therefore like the lung and the kidney of the earth, in large part because of phytoplankton's important role.

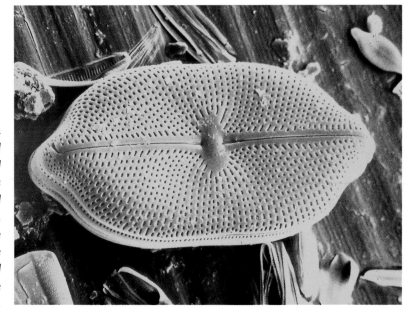

This diatom is called Navicula monilifera. *It has been enlarged 1,055 times. This cone-shaped algae, called pennate, is mobile. Its shell is decorated with innumerable small holes, and the longitudinal fissure that crosses it through the middle enables the living cell inside to "flow," whereby the whole body can move.*

This rosette with its regular spokelike rays is the shell, or frustule, of a diatom, of the Cyclotella meneghiniara *enlarged 1,800 times with the SEM. It lives in salt water. Some of these perfectly symmetrical algae look like cylindrical boxes with their covers and bases fitting into one another.*

The diatoms or bacillariophyta make up the majority of plant plankton. They grow and live 83 feet below the surface of the sea, where the blue rays of the specter sun can penetrate. Like plants, they contain chlorophyll and are able to synthesize living material from solar energy. But like animals, some of these species have the additional ability to move about.

The diatoms often coexist with the dinoflagellata or peridinians. This other large group of algae, brown-colored and single-celled, also have both animal and plant characteristics. They can sometimes be covered with cellulose walls that form sort of protective exterior skeletons. They move about and feed normally using two "whips" that are perpendicular to each other. Diatoms and dinoflagellata are often used to feed oysters raised in oyster parks.

Unfortunately, the beauty of these algae can't be seen by the naked eye. These single-celled beings are protected by a shell made of pectin and silica. These tiny shells are decorated with gorgeous embossed patterns: stripes, pearls, or scallops, depending on how the mineral penetrated them.

Is this a plant or a modern sculpture?

Those creatures who live off us!

There are miniature monsters living in the human environment of the temperate zones. And monster is not too strong a word, although they have familiar names: caterpillar, butterfly, flea, moth, etc. However small the living creature, all have predators and parasites. Thus, this caterpillar of the white cabbage moth, a formidable parasite of crops, is also able to house 150 parasite guests that live off it. The small animal is a reflection of a big one, a whole world unto itself.

What does this photo show?
Could it be a field of giant cactus?

The hatching of the eggs of a butterfly, the Pieris brassicae, which often wreaks havoc in our fields, better known as the white cabbage moth. This huge white butterfly lays eggs on cabbage, colza, and beet leaves. It hibernates in the pupal stage, an intermediary stage between the larva and the developed insect, and reproduces one or two generations a year. The food requirements of this caterpillar are very important. It is at this stage of its life that the insect destroys crops. Opposite left is a caterpillar, enlarged 50 times, just emerging from its egg.

THOSE CREATURES THAT LIVE OFF US

Man never lives alone.

hosts. They often parasitize several successive beings before reaching their adult size.

Who is this tiny creature from another world balancing a strange-looking parasol on the end of its trunk?
It's a Acanthrocirrus retriostris, or more commonly, a tapeworm. The one in this photograph has been enlarged 611 times. This tapeworm was removed from the body of a Canadian goose while encysted in the larval stage. Larvae only develop in the intestines of their

Certain beings are linked intimately to our body without our even suspecting their presence. . . . Others, in contrast, make themselves loudly known. The louse is a parasite hard to ignore and very unpleasant to live with! It lives on the scalp but also enjoys moving about in our forests of long hair! It reproduces extremely quickly: The female lays several dozen eggs a day! Once hatched, the baby lice reach adulthood in two weeks and can, in their turn, reproduce. The bites of these tiny insects (about .08 inch in size) cause severe itching. Although the adult lice move quickly and are sometimes hard to catch, the eggs can easily be seen; they grip onto the hair in small white clusters. Although lice were once nearly eradicated from schools, today they seem to be back in full force. This phenomenon can be explained by the fact that parasites have been able to build up resistance to the commonly used insecticides containing pyrethrin.

As for the tapeworm, it causes even more trouble. Its eggs, invisible to the naked eye, can often be found in raw or partly cooked meat. If we eat it, we absorb the parasite. Because it has no digestive apparatus, the tapeworm eats the food that's already been digested. In order to do that, it settles in the intestines by using tiny hooks. These hooks are attached to the end of the rostellum, a small beak-like protrusion on the tapeworm's head. The animal can withdraw the rostellum into its head or, alternately, can insert it into the intestinal tissue of its host. The four holes above the rostellum are not eyes but powerful suction cups. The body of the worm is a series of rings and can reach the length of 89 feet.

Pediculus humanus capitis, or the scalp louse, enlarged 205 times. This parasite has fastened itself to a hair. We can see the strong nails of its 6 claws. There are three types of lice that live as parasites on humans: the scalp louse (measuring .08 to .1 inch), the body louse (measuring .12 to .14 inch), and the crab louse (measuring .06 inch).

THE ENEMIES OF PLANTS

Everyone has seen news reports about those gigantic clouds of locusts that regularly ravage African crops. Often this plague of locusts hits populations that are already destitute, leaving in their wake famine and despair. In our part of the world, agriculture's worst enemy is not necessarily the biggest. Whether it is aphids in barley, wheat, or in oats, cochineal in citrus orchards, thrips in greenhouses, weevils or moths, the scenario is the same—entire harvests destroyed, the work of a whole year gone, farmers gone bankrupt, serious economic losses, sometimes affecting a whole country. The weevil, for example, can be particularly destructive. This minuscule (.12 to .16 inch long), rather comical-looking beetle is a real scourge. In one year several generations can multiply in cereal stock. Entire storehouses of wheat grains, flour, or semolina can be infested in a very short time. However, the use of fumigant insecticides and better methods of storing grains have helped control the insect ravages.

The problem is that pesticides—these chemical products especially created to fight the animal or plant parasites that prey on crops—are dangerous, expensive, and polluting to the environment. What then is left to us to fight this scourge of insects that has come from an ecological disequilibrium? The biological battle.

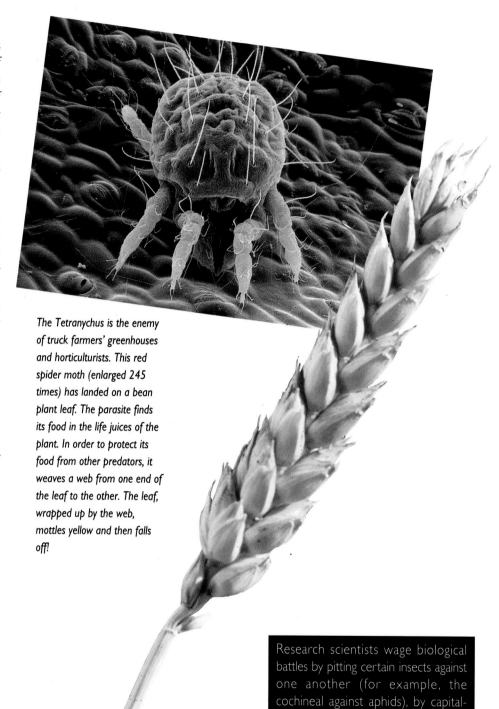

The Tetranychus is the enemy of truck farmers' greenhouses and horticulturists. This red spider moth (enlarged 245 times) has landed on a bean plant leaf. The parasite finds its food in the life juices of the plant. In order to protect its food from other predators, it weaves a web from one end of the leaf to the other. The leaf, wrapped up by the web, mottles yellow and then falls off!

Research scientists wage biological battles by pitting certain insects against one another (for example, the cochineal against aphids), by capitalizing on natural predatory instincts to fight against the phenomenon of insect invasions, which itself is the result of a disturbance in the natural order of things. Scientists have found a predator to the Tetranychus. It is a tiny moth, the *Phyloseiulus persimilis*, being raised in laboratories for eventual commercial use.

When tiny creatures create great havoc . . .

This Granarius sitophilus, or wheat weevil, thrives in grain. The insect has been enlarged 60 times in this photograph. Its head terminates in a rostrum and is equipped with sharp mandibles. The rostrum perforates the fibrous envelope of the wheat grain, which is then ground up by the mandibles. The female weevil is a parasite that is very sensitive to cold and therefore is found most often in hot climates.

41

THE SMALLEST OF ANIMALS

Copulation of two ticks, enlarged 19 times. The tick (or ixodid) is an acarien. It belongs to the large Arachnides family, which includes spiders and scorpions. The tick sucks the blood of mammals—dogs, cats, sheep, horses, or even man! It also attacks birds, snakes, and lizards by attaching itself to the thinnest part of their skins, swelling up once it has sucked its fill of blood. Unlike the leech, it remains embedded in the skin. Pulling it out carelessly can be dangerous because its buccale parts (or mouth parts) will tear apart and cause an inflammation of the sore. This parasite lives in pastures, undergrowth, and bushes.

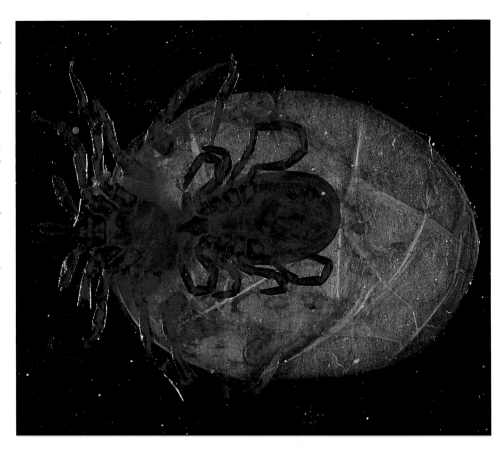

The animal world seems to know only two relationships with the Other (which at times can be confused with one another): parasitism and predation. The parasite, such as the tapeworm, the louse, or the tick, live off their host without causing enough damage to kill it. In contrast, the predator kills its victim for food (as in the case of spiders with flies and cochineals with aphids). This "law of the jungle" seems to apply to small as well as large animals. But it seems that the smaller the animals, the stranger, the more subtle, the odder their strategy. For example, a recent discovery has shown that certain spiders weave their web in a flowerlike form using a special sort of silk that is better able to reflect the ultraviolet rays of sunlight. And why? To better trap nectar-gathering insects that perceive ultraviolet light and in order to find flowers!

In the animal world there does exist a third type of relationship to the Other: symbiosis. This is an association of two species that can't live, or would at least live with much greater difficulty, without their mutual interdependence. There are many cases of different degrees of symbiosis in nature: the clown fish and the sea anemone; the lichen, which is the association of an alga and a fungus; or, on the scale of the infinitely tiny, the bacteria that live in our digestive tract and that help us to assimilate our food. Symbiosis is what we humans could call "a good contract": something that works to the mutual advantage of both parties.

Only three species of Braulides similar to the one shown on the opposite page are known. As an adult, this fly (enlarged 350 times) lives off the queen bee, feeding from the nectar that it takes directly from the bee's mouth! The larva prefers to feed on the wax that contains the pollen or on that which covers the honeycomb cells. Each to his or her own taste!

This minuscule insect (enlarged 240 times) hanging with all its claws to the hair of its host is a fly parasite to the honeybee, the *Braula coeca*. Over evolutionary time, it has lost the use of its wings and has developed clawlike legs that look somewhat like combs. To get about, its grasping claws slide along the bee hairs.

THE UNINVITED GUESTS IN THE HOUSE

I f we think that asphalt, cement, windows, paving stones, and rugs isolate our houses and keep them separate from nature, we have a surprise in store for us! And we're not talking about flies, wasps, or mosquitoes, our "temporary" visitors, but rather the permanent "squatters," inhabitants who live with us without our knowing it. Our entrance hall, where we keep our coats and jackets, is the home for several little creatures: the brown moth, who just loves snacking on wool and fur, the spotted dermestes, and the clothes moth, all insects that are also fond of material and furs. Libraries and offices have their own "guests": the psocid, also called the book louse, or the death-watch beetle, which loves wood.

If you look under the sink in the kitchen, you might very well see little insects called silverfish. While peering behind the radiator, you might find little fire mites. In the pantry near the cheeses is where the cheese mite loves to settle. The meal moths love to be on smooth walls, while the tabby moth, an eclectic gourmand who loves not only material and

The acarids share the territory of the house. The Tyroglyphus proliferate on cheeses, the Cheylatus attack old clothes, furs, and feathers. The specimens contained in the dust of a house (as much as 850,500 specimens per ounce) are then studied in detail, because the excrement left by them causes the majority of allergic asthmas.

feathers but also everything we eat, only occasionally passes through the kitchen but doesn't like to stay there. It prefers the dampness of the cellar, along with its companion, the cork mite. As for our nice soft beds, they are also nice and comfy for a microscopic acarid and its big family—in one bed there might be over two million insects! There they have a constant

The head of a butterfly, the Plutella xyhostella, enlarged 68 times. It lives in material, grain—and food. This tiny moth—about .24 inches long — has a body covered with very fine scales. Its eyes (right in the center of the photo) are enormous, and its antenna is segmented. The larva of this insect develops on food products.

source of food, for they feed on the dead cells continually being shed from our bodies.

Bed acarid (bed mite, enlarged 1,105 times) belong to the family of Dermatophagoides (literally: skin eaters!). The animal has been isolated from a sample of household dust. It has very long, spiny hair, which enables it to grip onto dust or tiny objects in its environment. This acarida molts frequently, shedding its fragile and lightweight remains into the atmosphere.

WHEN A MOSQUITO CAN SEEM AS GIGANTIC AS AN OX!

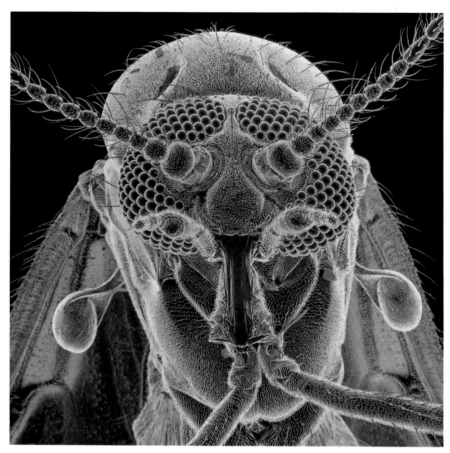

This photo of an insect (enlarged 120 times) is not the work of an imaginative artist, nor is it an extraterrestrial being! It's just a mosquito, measuring less than .2 inch. The long, pearly appendices at the top of the photo are its antennae, and below them are sensorial organs, the feelers, which are used for grasping and tasting. The trunk that the insect uses to feed itself is between the feelers.

Mask of a character from the film Starcrash

In front of these monsters, the imagination hesitates: Are these devils from a carnival? Marionettes from a nightmare? A model set for horror films? The two enlargements on these pages are of two of Mother Nature's "children," two creatures well known to everyone. They are simply mosquitoes! Those who make masks or who create science-fiction characters don't have to look any further to find their inspiration!

We all hate mosquitoes! First because of their bites and second because of the buzzing noise they make right in our ears when we're trying to get to sleep on hot summer nights. They are irritating all right, but what is merely irritating in our temperate regions can become, in other latitudes, deadly, for mosquitoes can carry dangerous viruses such as malaria, yellow fever, and elephantiasis. Therefore, it is difficult to find the mosquito a very appealing creature—at least until its marvels are seen under the scanning microscope!

The little philosopher Yoda from Star Wars, *a film by George Lucas*

The mosquito appears bigger than an ox. Its anatomy is absolutely amazing, unimaginable. The form and position of its organs defy common sense: its eyes envelop its head, its legs seem to emerge from its nose and its eyes, the thorax overhangs the head, its antennae have feathers, its "mouth" looks like a snout. Who would have thought a study of the simple mosquito would reveal so many astonishing discoveries? What do you think of it? Beautiful? Frightening? Fascinating? It's up to you to decide!

The photograph above is of E.T., the famous extraterrestrial from Steven Spielberg's science fiction film of the same name. And the creature in the photo below, does it really exist in nature? No, it is also from a film. This hideous head was created for David Cronenberg's film The Fly.

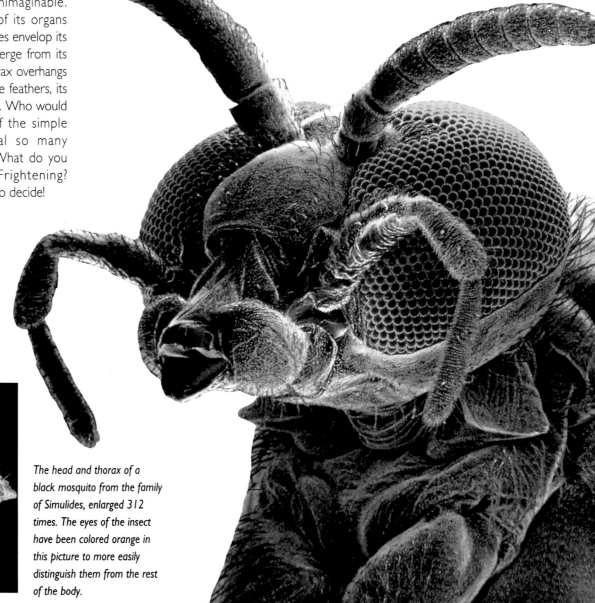

The head and thorax of a black mosquito from the family of Simulides, enlarged 312 times. The eyes of the insect have been colored orange in this picture to more easily distinguish them from the rest of the body.

PHOTO CREDITS

Special thanks to the following people and organizations who helped make this book possible:

- The Jéol Company and its Commercial Director, Mr. Michot
- The CRA Rhôe-Poulenc, and particularly Daniel Bemelin, Bernard Boudot, René Ayrôles and his team
- The I.R.S.I.D., particularly Mrs. D. Benoit, Pierrè Chemelle, Daniel Boulou, and Serge Steer
- The IRHO-CIRAD, particularly Mr. Roch Desmier de Chenon

Design and Layout: Etienne Hénocq - François Huertas

New Discovery Books
Macmillan Publishing Company
866 Third Avenue
New York, NY 10022

Maxwell Macmillan Canada, Inc.
1200 Eglinton Avenue East
Suite 200
Don Mills, Ontario M3C 3N1

Macmillan Publishing Company is part of the Maxwell Communication Group of Companies.

First Edition

Printed in the United States of America

10 9 8 7 6 5 4 3 2 1

ISBN 0-02-718650-4
Library of Congress Catalog Card Number 93-9337